Paw Prints

Dachshunds

by Kaitlyn Duling

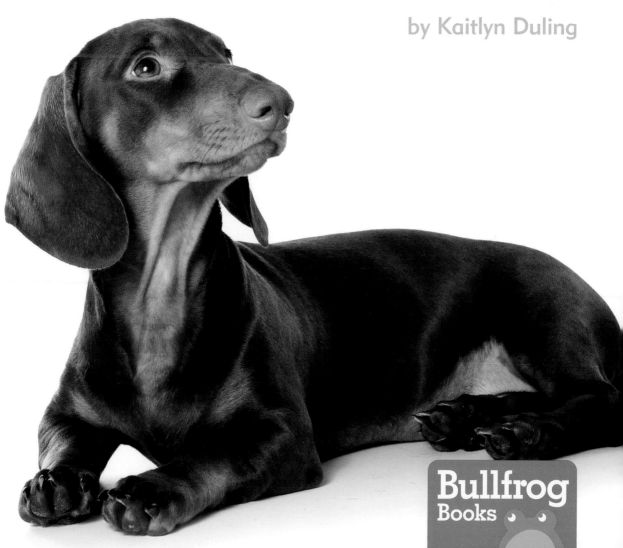

Bullfrog Books

Ideas for Parents and Teachers

Bullfrog Books let children practice reading informational text at the earliest reading levels. Repetition, familiar words, and photo labels support early readers.

Before Reading

- Discuss the cover photo. What does it tell them?

- Look at the picture glossary together. Read and discuss the words.

Read the Book

- "Walk" through the book and look at the photos. Let the child ask questions. Point out the photo labels.

- Read the book to the child, or have him or her read independently.

After Reading

- Prompt the child to think more. Ask: Have you ever seen a dachshund? Would you like to play with one?

This book is for Vada, Mayim, James, and Stella Peterson.

Bullfrog Books are published by Jump!
5357 Penn Avenue South
Minneapolis, MN 55419
www.jumplibrary.com

Library of Congress Cataloging-in-Publication Data

Names: Duling, Kaitlyn, author.
Title: Dachshunds / by Kaitlyn Duling.
Description: Minneapolis, MN : Jump!, Inc., 2018.
Series: Paw prints | Series: Bullfrog books
Includes index.
Audience: Ages 5 to 8. | Audience: Grades K to 3.
Identifiers: LCCN 2017039654 (print)
LCCN 2017043176 (ebook)
ISBN 9781624967696 (ebook)
ISBN 9781624967689 (hardcover : alk. paper)
Subjects: LCSH: Dachshunds—Juvenile literature.
Classification: LCC SF429.D25 (ebook)
LCC SF429.D25 D85 2018 (print) | DDC 636.753/8—dc23
LC record available at https://lccn.loc.gov/2017039654

Editor: Jenna Trnka
Book Designer: Molly Ballanger

Photo Credits: Jagodka/Shutterstock, cover; Utekhina Anna/Shutterstock, 1; Ivanova N/Shutterstock, 3; Grossemy Vanessa/Alamy, 4; Ondrej83/Shutterstock, 5; Max Allen/Shutterstock, 6, 23tl; Top-Pet-Pics/Alamy, 6–7; WilleeCole/iStock, 8; bestjeroen/Adobe Stock, 9; Liliya Kulianionak/Shutterstock, 10–11, 14–15, 18–19, 23mr, 23br; oxilixo/iStock, 12–13; Eric Isselee/Shutterstock, 14 (left); cynoclub/Shutterstock, 15, 23ml; Marta Nardini/Getty, 16–17, 23tr; paylessimages/iStock, 20–21; Masarik/Shutterstock, 22; justsolove/Shutterstock, 23bl; Csanad Kiss/Shutterstock, 24.

Printed in the United States of America at Corporate Graphics in North Mankato, Minnesota.

Table of Contents

Long and Low

Look at that long dog!

It is very short.

It has a silly name.
Dachshund!

They came from Germany.

Their name means "badger dog."

They hunted badgers.

They can fit in holes.

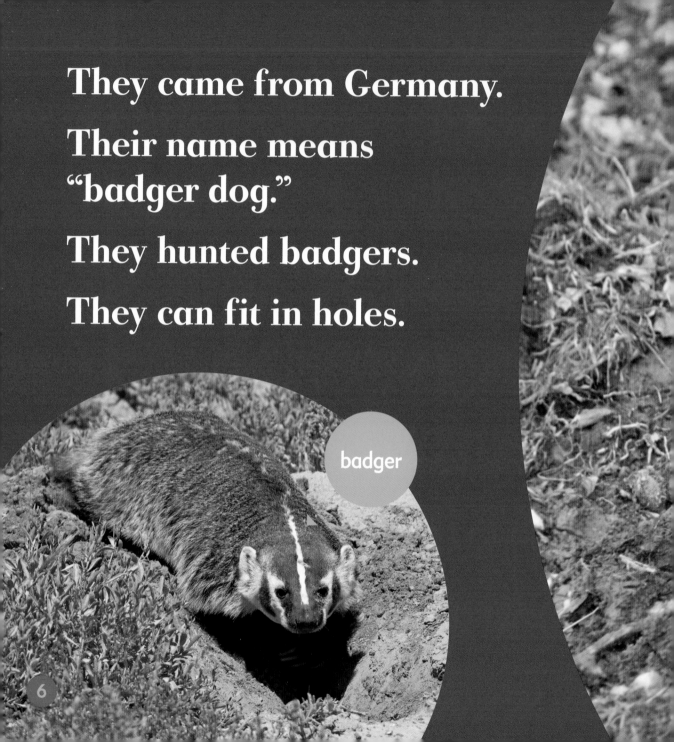

badger

She has a great
sense of smell.

She smells something.

Watch her dig!

These dogs are short.
Some are extra small.
They are miniature.

miniature

They can be many different colors.

Black. Tan. Brown.

13

Their coats are different, too.

Smooth. Long. Wire.
Which kind of
hair do you like?

coat

15

These dogs are very smart.

They are loyal, too.

They love their owners.

They are spunky!
They love to play.

Do you want to play with one?

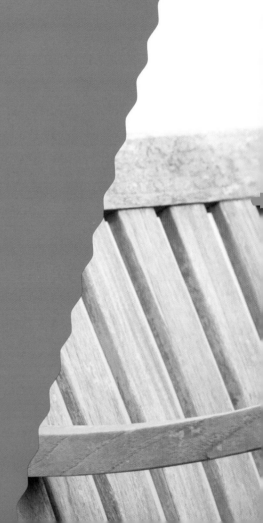

A Dachshund Up Close

snout

ear

coat

paw

Picture Glossary

badgers
Animals that burrow in the ground.

loyal
Faithful.

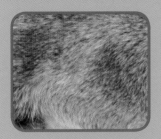

coats
Dogs' fur.

miniature
A smaller version of something.

Germany
A country in Western Europe.

spunky
Courageous and determined.

Index

To Learn More

Learning more is as easy as 1, 2, 3.

1) Go to www.factsurfer.com

2) Enter "dachshunds" into the search box.

3) Click the "Surf" button to see a list of websites.

With factsurfer.com, finding more information is just a click away.